C0-DAQ-708

Reflections

by

Melinda Malone

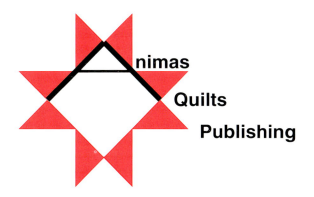

Animas
Quilts
Publishing

600 Main Ave.
Durango, CO 81301
(303) 247-2582

Meet the Author.....

Melinda Malone grew up in the small southwest Kansas farming community of Ulysses. She has been interested in crafts all her life, discovering the joy of quilting in 1989. She and sons Seth and Adam now make their home in Bayfield, Colorado. Upon moving to this area, Melinda discovered Animas Quilts in Durango. She soon began teaching quilting classes. The winters in Colorado provided her with the long evenings during which she began her first efforts of designing her own quilts.

ACKNOWLEDGEMENTS

My sincere appreciation goes to some of my quilting buddies: Sue Andresen, Mary Dent, Kim Gjere, Barbara Morgan, Sue Ann Schwiller and Becky Smith. They have been so generous with their time and talents, bringing to life in fabric many of the designs herein.

Special appreciation goes to my sons, Seth and Adam. Their interest, encouragement and opinions were some of the ways in which they participated in this book. I thank them for their patience as I struggled with the work involved in putting this together. Also, a big thank you to my family for words of encouragement and support.

    Melinda Malone

Reflections

Copyright © 1993 by Melinda Malone
Animas Quilts Publishing
Durango, CO 81301

Front Cover: Cinnamon Twist, pg. 34
  by Melinda Malone and Barbara Morgan
Back Cover: Summer Sparkler, pg. 25
  by Melinda Malone

All rights reserved. Printed in the United States of America.
No part of this book may be reproduced in any manner
without the express written permission of the author.

CREDITS:	
Editor	Kim Gjere
Asst. Editor	Barbara Morgan
Graphics	Jackie Robinson
Photographer	Chris Marona

The original design for this book is a result of some classes I have taken from others and their insistence that we get our ideas down on paper. I began designing during the evening hours of the winter of 1992. While my family watched television in the evening, I would sit with my graph paper and pencil and sketch. It was from those first few sketches that this design developed. In the fall of 1992 I made the first quilt in the series, Reflections. With encouragement to continue "playing" with the design, the original has evolved into a series of quilts that use the theme of two color values to create eye pleasing designs. They are fun to make and appealing to quilt makers and quilt lovers alike. The simple design gives each quilter the opportunity to use his/her own creativity because the "set" options are limitless. Use your imagination to experiment with these designs and experience the pleasure that comes when you incorporate your own ideas into your quilting projects.

GETTING STARTED

You'll need these basic supplies to make your work easier:

- Rotary Cutter
- Cutting Mat
- Ruler
- Quick Quarter II®
- Binding Miter Tool®
- Scissors
- Thread snips
- Ball-point pen which doesn't bleed or a fabric marker
- Thread - neutral color
- Sewing Machine - cleaned and oiled

SELECTING FABRIC - <u>IMPORTANT!</u>

Choose fabrics which are high quality, 100% cotton, as your piecing will be easier and more accurate. The yardages listed in the charts allow for maximum shrinkage on 44" wide cotton fabric plus a small allowance.

As I was working with the fabric for these designs, it quickly became clear to me that fabric selection is the key to a visual success with these designs. The "KEY" being that two distinct values of fabric are chosen, a dark and a light. Medium value colors DO NOT WORK in this quilt. It is the true dark / light combinations that are effective. Any time there is a doubt about whether there will be enough contrast, you probably do not have enough contrast. There should be NO DOUBT!

When selecting a fabric with a large print, all the colors represented in the large print MUST contrast with the other fabric chosen. My experience with these designs taught me to be especially careful in selecting the other contrasting fabric. Don't exclude large prints in your fabric selections, but choose carefully so that your quilt is a visual success!

Since we are working with dark and light fabrics, it might be good to remind you to "set" the colors in the dark fabrics. This is done easily by adding 1-1/2 cups of salt to a washer filled with COLD water. Let the fabric soak in the salt water mixture overnight. Rinse until the water rinses clear. DO NOT use detergents when you pretreat new fabric as it washes out the sizing. Wash with clear water and dry at a hot temperature to obtain the maximum shrinkage before cutting your quilt. Always press your fabric before cutting. If your fabric has lost its sizing, use a spray fabric finish as you press.

GENERAL INSTRUCTIONS

CUTTING YOUR FABRIC

Fold your 44" wide fabric like it came off the bolt. The selvages will be together and will run lengthwise of your fabric. Place the fabric on your cutting mat and bring the folded edge up and even with the selvage edges. Now your fabric is folded so it is four layers thick and it measures about 11" in width. Clean cut the raw edge of the fabric using a ruler and a rotary cutter and you are ready to begin cutting. Specific cutting instructions are included with each quilt.

NOTE: Before you begin sewing, practice on some scraps to get an exact 1/4" seam allowance. With all the triangles and different units in this quilt, things will go together much easier if your seam allowance is exact and consistent throughout construction.

HALF SQUARE TRIANGLES

Half square triangles (HSTs) are the basis for most of the blocks in this book. There are several ways to make these and I will describe two of them.

You can make HSTs by drawing a grid onto your fabric. Add 7/8" to the <u>finished</u> size of the HST needed. Draw a grid of squares this measurement onto the back of the light piece of fabric which is right sides together with the darker piece of fabric. The quilts in this book use 1-1/2" finished HSTs making your grid 2-3/8". Summer Sparkler also uses 2" HSTs in the corner blocks and the grid for them will be 2-7/8". You will need half as many squares drawn as the number of HSTs required, as each square yields two HSTs. Draw diagonal lines through the grid, in both directions, then stitch 1/4" on both sides of the diagonal lines over the entire grid.

A.

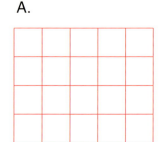

B.

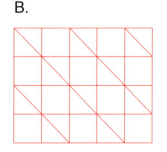

C.

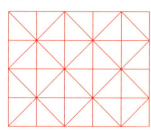

D.

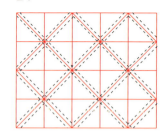

Cut on the vertical, horizontal and diagonal lines of the grid, and you have your HSTs. Clip the corners and press toward the dark fabric.

There are products on the market which have simplified this procedure. I used pre-printed triangle paper to make the quilts in this book. It already has the grid drawn. Use the 1-1/2" size except for the corner blocks on Summer Sparkler which require the 2" size.

Refer to the half square triangle chart for the quilt you have chosen to make. Cut the number of rows needed from the triangle paper (we figured the 1-1/2" size with four squares per row, the 2" size with two per row). Work with nine or fewer rows at a time to keep things easy to handle. Then cut the 10" (7" for the 2" size HST) strips of fabric in the colors needed the length of the paper. Lay the two fabrics right sides together, then lay the HST paper on top. Use straight pins to secure the layers together. Stitch, using a very small stitch length setting (this perforates the paper so that it comes off the fabric easier) following the dotted lines. Cut apart on the solid lines. Press the HST toward the dark fabric.

<u>TIMESAVER HINT:</u> *Cut on the solid lines so that you have squares with the paper on. Fold the paper on the stitched lines and tear away both sides. Gently tug on the fabric corners only, which will "pop" the center strip of paper loose and remove. Then fold the square in half and clip the corners off to eliminate the little fabric tips from creating bulky seams. Cut down the center, between stitching lines.*

GIANT HALF SQUARE TRIANGLES

Giant half square triangles are used in blocks 7, 11, and 13. Use 5-3/8" squares of light and dark. Layer one square of each color, right sides together. Place the Quick Quarter tool diagonally on the light fabric and draw a line on both sides of the tool. Stitch on these lines and cut down the center. Press the seams toward the darker piece.

STAR POINT UNITS

Star Point units are made from squares which measure 1-1/4" greater than the desired finished size of the unit. In other words, a 1-1/2" Star Point unit begins as 2-3/4" squares of the two fabrics which make up that unit. On the wrong side of the lighter of these two pieces draw a diagonal line exactly from one corner to the opposite corner. Layer the two squares of fabric right sides together, with the line on top. Stitch precisely 1/4" on both sides of the line. The tool called a Quick Quarter II by Quilter's Rule makes this easier. Place it diagonally on the light fabric and draw a line on both sides of the Quick Quarter tool. Stitch on these lines. Cut along the center, trim the corners and press the seams toward the darker piece.

Timesaver Hint: Use pre-printed Triangle Paper designed for 1-1/2" Star Point Units!

Layer two pieced units right sides together, seams interlocking and opposite colors on top of each other. Place the Quick Quarter tool on the wrong side of a pieced square, perpendicular to the seam. Draw along both sides. Stitch accurately on the lines and cut apart down the center. Trim the corner points and press the seams to one side. This makes two Star Point units.

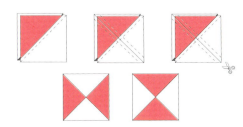

SUPER STAR POINT UNITS

Super Star Point units are three parts one color and one part the other color.

Begin as you make a Star Point unit by making pieced squares from two 2-3/4" squares of different colors. Layer a pieced square right sides together on top of a 2-3/8" square of fabric. The pieced square and the plain square will be the same size. Draw diagonal lines on the wrong side of the pieced square unit, perpendicular to the seam, as done for the Star Point units. Stitch, cut down the center, and press.

BLOCK CONSTRUCTION

When the HSTs, Star Point units and Super Star Point units are cut and sewn, begin piecing the blocks. What follows is a detailed description for constructing each block in this book. The individual quilt directions will refer to this section for these instructions. The measurements for the pieces in this section will include seam allowances, that is they are the exact size that you cut them.

All of the blocks are similar in that the center of the block is constructed first. It is generally a 9-patch block (nine 2" squares sewn in three rows of three). Some blocks have 2" x 3-1/2" rectangles which replace two 2" blocks in the 9-patch section. Blocks 7, 9, and 11 have a Giant HST in the center. For each block the pieces needed to construct the block are listed. There are drawings showing how to sew it together.

Lay out the components in the center 9-patch part of each block, making sure the HSTs and Star Point units are turned the right direction. <u>Don't get careless — it's very easy to get these pieces turned the wrong way.</u> Sew them together in rows, and the rows together, alternating the seams so they will lie flat.

"Frame" the 9-patch centers by sewing on the side segments. Finally sew the top and bottom "frames" on. Press gently, being careful not to stretch.

You may wish to use assembly line construction by sewing the first step for all of a particular block before continuing on to the next step. Thus, if you are making 20 of Block #1 you would sew 20 light Super Star Point units to 20 HSTs before moving to the next step.

NOTE: All HSTs are light / dark combinations unless listed otherwise.

BLOCK #1

block 1

- five HSTs
- two each light and dark
    Super Star Point units
- one each light and dark
    2" x 2" squares
- one each light and dark
    2" x 5" rectangles
- one each light and dark
    2" x 6-1/2" rectangles

BLOCK #2

block 2

- five HSTs
- one each light and dark
    2" x 2" squares
- one each light and dark
    2" x 3-1/2" rectangles
- one each light and dark
    2" x 5" rectangles
- one each light and dark
    2" x 6-1/2" rectangles

BLOCK #2A - This block is like block #2 except that light / accent HSTs are substituted for the light / dark HSTs

- five light / accent HSTs
- one each light and dark
    2" x 2" squares

block 2a

- one each light and dark
    2" x 3-1/2" rectangles
- one each light and dark
    2" x 5" rectangles
- one each light and dark
    2" x 6-1/2" rectangles

BLOCK #3 - This block is constructed the same as block #2. Two light / accent HSTs are used in place of two light / dark HSTs.

block 3

- three light / dark HSTs
- two light / accent HSTs
- one each light and dark
    2" x 2" squares
- one each light and dark
    2" x 3-1/2" rectangles
- one each light and dark
    2" x 5" rectangles
- one each light and dark
    2" x 6-1/2" rectangles

BLOCK #3A - This is the same as above except that the different color HSTs have traded places.

- two light / dark HSTs
- three light / accent HSTs
- one each light and dark
    2" x 2" squares

block 3a

- one each light and dark
    2" x 3-1/2" rectangles
- one each light and dark
    2" x 5" rectangles
- one each light and dark
    2" x 6-1/2" rectangles

BLOCK #4 - This block is like block #3 with accent pieces taking the place of dark and vice versa.

- three light / accent HSTs
- two light / dark HSTs
- one each light and accent
    2" x 2" squares

block 4

- one each light and accent
    2" x 3-1/2" rectangles
- one each light and accent
    2" x 5" rectangles
- one each light and accent
    2" x 6-1/2" rectangles

BLOCK #4A - The same as #4 with the HSTs reversing positions.

- two light / accent HSTs
- three light / dark HSTs
- one each light and accent
    2" x 2" squares

block 4a

- one each light and accent
    2" x 3-1/2" rectangles
- one each light and accent
    2" x 5" rectangles
- one each light and accent
    2" x 6-1/2" rectangles

BLOCK #5

seven HSTs
two each light and dark
    Super Star Point units
one each light and dark
    2" x 2" squares
three each light and dark
    2" x 3-1/2" rectangles

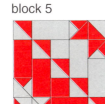
block 5

BLOCK #6 - Be extra careful to get all the colors in the right places!

two accent 1 / dark HSTs
two accent 1 / accent 2 HSTs
two accent 2 / light HSTs
three light / dark HSTs
one each light and dark
    2" x 2" squares
two each light and dark
    2" x 3-1/2" rectangles
one each light and dark
    2" x 5" rectangles

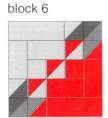
block 6

BLOCK #7 - Note also #11 except for the colors of the small HSTs

one giant HST
   (cut 5-3/8")
two accent 1 / accent 2 HSTs
two accent 1 / dark HSTs
two accent 2 / light HSTs
one each light and dark
    2" x 3-1/2" rectangles
one each light and dark
    2" x 5" rectangles

block 7

BLOCK #8

five HSTs
two each light and dark Super
    Star Point units
one each light and dark
    2" x 2" squares
one each light and dark
    2" x 5" rectangles
one each light and dark
    2" x 6-1/2" rectangles

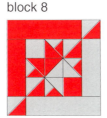
block 8

BLOCK #8A - This block is identical to the #8 block except that light / accent HSTs are in the corners instead of light/ dark HSTs.

three light / dark HSTs
two light / accent HSTs
two each light and dark
    Super Star Point units
one each light and dark
    2" x 2" squares
one each light and dark
    2" x 5" rectangles
one each light and dark
    2" x 6-1/2" rectangles

block 8a

BLOCK #9

seven HSTs
two each light and dark
    Super Star Point units
one each light and dark
    2" x 2" squares
two each light and dark
    2" x 5" rectangles

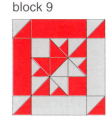
block 9

BLOCK #10

eleven HSTs
one each light and dark
    2" x 5" rectangles
one each light and dark
    2" x 6-1/2" rectangles

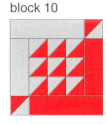
block 10

BLOCK #11

one giant HST (cut 5-3/8")
six HSTs
one each light and dark
    2" x 3-1/2" rectangles
one each light and dark
    2" x 5" rectangles

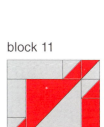
block 11

BLOCK #12

eight HSTs
one Star Point unit
two each light and dark
    Super Star Point units
two each light and dark
    2" x 5" rectangles

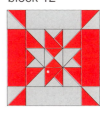
block 12

BLOCK #13

one giant HST (cut 5-3/8")
two HSTs
one each light and dark
    2" x 5" rectangles
one each light and dark
    2" x 6-1/2" rectangles

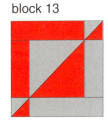

block 13

BLOCK #14

eight HSTs
one Star Point unit
two each light and dark
    Super Star Point units
two each light and dark
    2" x 5" rectangles

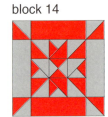

block 14

BLOCK #14A - This block is the same as block #14
except that four light / accent HSTs are used in the corners.

four light / dark HSTs
four light / accent HSTs
one Star Point unit
two each light and dark
    Super Star Point units
two each light and dark
    2" x 5" rectangles

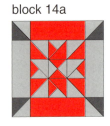

block 14a

This concludes the blocks used in the quilts featured in this book. While designing and planning the quilts several other blocks were designed and drawings of them are below. You may want to use them to create your own "reflection".

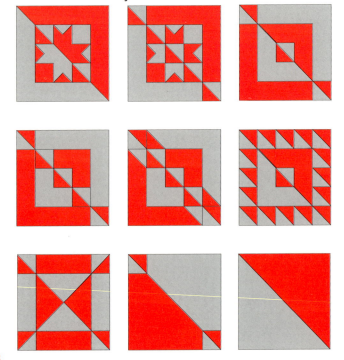

ASSEMBLY OF BLOCKS - Pairs of Pairs Pickup

Sew the blocks into horizontal pairs. Then sew the pairs to the adjacent pair below them (Pairs of Pairs). When joining these watch the seams so they go opposite directions. Continue sewing sections together until the top is assembled. Be sure to match the <u>seam lines</u> of the blocks if they are not the same size and let the excess or shortage be at the ends.

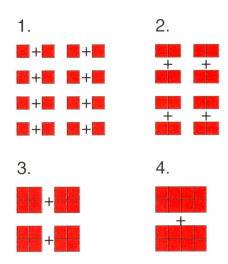

BORDERS

All of the quilts have suggested borders. I would especially encourage you to be creative at this point. Borders can be fun! Use the suggested borders as just that, and feel free to individualize your quilt here! The cutting instructions with each quilt will tell you exactly the width and number of strips to cut from each fabric. Begin by sewing the border strips together, end to end, with a 1/2" seam allowance. As you attach them to the quilt be careful not to stretch them. A good way to do this is to measure your quilt in the center, both vertically and horizontally, and cut borders accordingly, allowing for mitered corners if desired. Pin borders to quilt, easing in any fullness. Sew the side borders first, then the top and bottom. Sometimes I simply overlap the borders with straight seams across the previous edges. Other times I miter the corners. To miter easily sew the borders to the quilt top with a 1/4" seam, beginning and ending the stitching 1/4" from the edge of the quilt. Do not stitch through the seam allowances. Leave "tails" of border fabric extending at each end. These "tails" need to be a bit longer than they are wide. Press the seams of the borders toward the border (away from the quilt) then lay the corner on the ironing board with the border strips extending at the corners.

Take the border strip which is lying on top and fold it at the end of the stitching so it lies directly on top of the other border piece.

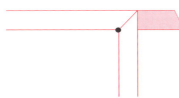

You can tell visually if this corner looks true. If so, press flat, which will put a crease in the top layer. Without disturbing their placement, carefully fold back the top border layer and stitch in the pressed crease. Examine your work. Trim the excess to 1/4" and press these seams open.

QUILTING

Decide how you want to quilt your Reflections Quilts. You can quilt 1/4" away from the seams, making triangles within the triangles; quilt in the ditch, which means sew in the seams; or put an entirely new pattern on top.

BINDING

My favorite binding is a doubled 3" strip of fabric cut on the straight of grain. Sew the 3" strips together, end to end, and press in half lengthwise, wrong sides together, so you have a long strip measuring 1-1/2" wide. Attach the binding to all four sides of the quilt, stitching through all the layers (top, batting and backing) matching the cut edge of the binding with the cut edge of the quilt, and leaving a 2" extension at each end. Use a

1/4" seam and a walking foot (even feed foot) on your machine. Begin sewing 1/4" from the end of the quilt and stop 1/4" from the other end. Repeat for all four sides. Do not sew through the seam allowances. Trim away the excess batting and backing, leaving about 1/2" of batting and backing showing on all four sides. This excess will stuff into the binding making it full.

To miter the corners of the binding fold the quilt on itself at the corner so the binding strips of two adjacent sides are laying one on top of the other. Create a 90° "V" toward the outer points of the binding by measuring carefully so both sides of the "V" are the same length. Mark the "V", stitch and trim. The Binding Miter Tool ® makes this even easier. Turn the binding to the back of the quilt and hand stitch into place.

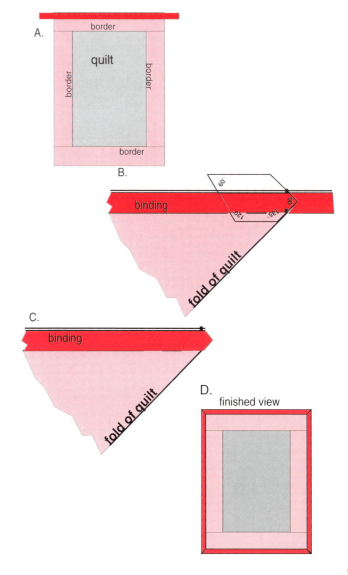

Wallhanging

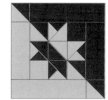

block 1

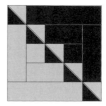

block 2

This is where it all begins. The original two blocks are used in this quilt and prove that a complicated design isn't necessary to make beautiful quilts! These two blocks can be arranged in many different sets. Here are two sets plus a challenge for you to get your creative thoughts flowing and get sewing!

YARDAGE:

	Wallhanging 57" x 57" (6 x 6 blocks)
Light Fabric	1-7/8 yds.
Dark Fabric	1-7/8 yds.
First Border	1/2 yd.
Second Border	7/8 yd.
Binding	5/8 yd.
Backing	3-1/2 yds.

	King 99" x 99" (10 x 10 blocks)
Light Fabric	4-1/4 yds.
Dark Fabric	4-1/4 yds.
First Border	1-1/2 yds.
Second Border	1/2 yd.
Third Border	2 yds.
Binding	1 yd.
Backing	8-7/8 yds.

CUTTING:

		Wallhanging	King
From <u>both</u> light & dark			
2" strips		14	38
into 2" x 6-1/2""		36	100
2" x 5"		36	100
2" x 3-1/2""		16	48
2" x 2"		36	100
2-3/8" strips		2	4
into 2-3/8" x 2-3/8"		20	52
2-3/4" strips		2	4
into 2-3/4" x 2-3/4"		20	52
10" strips		2	4
First border			
2-1/2" strips		5	
5-1/2" strips			9
Second border:			
4-1/4" strips		6	
1-1/2" strips			9
Third border:			
6-1/2" strips			10
Binding:			
3" strips		6	10

CONSTRUCTION:

MAKE HSTs according to the general instructions on page 4. Make the amount shown below using the 10" strips of fabric previously cut. *(Remember to make half as many squares as needed because one square makes two HSTs.)*

Light/Dark	# HSTs	# rows HST paper
Wallhanging	180	23 rows
King	500	63 rows

MAKE SUPER STAR POINT UNITS. Use the 2-3/8" and 2-3/4" squares already cut and refer to page 5 in the General Instructions. You need 40 each of light and dark units for the Wallhanging and 104 each for the King.

ASSEMBLE BLOCKS according to the following chart, using the directions on page 6.

	Block #1	Block #2
Wallhanging	20	16
King	52	48

ARRANGE THE BLOCKS according to the diagram (see page 10 for the Wallhanging and page 11 for the King). Sew the blocks together using the Pairs of Pairs method described on page 8.

SEW THE BORDERS on referring to page 8 for a discussion of borders.

QUILT THE TOP as you wish, then add binding using the 3" strips cut earlier and the directions on page 9.

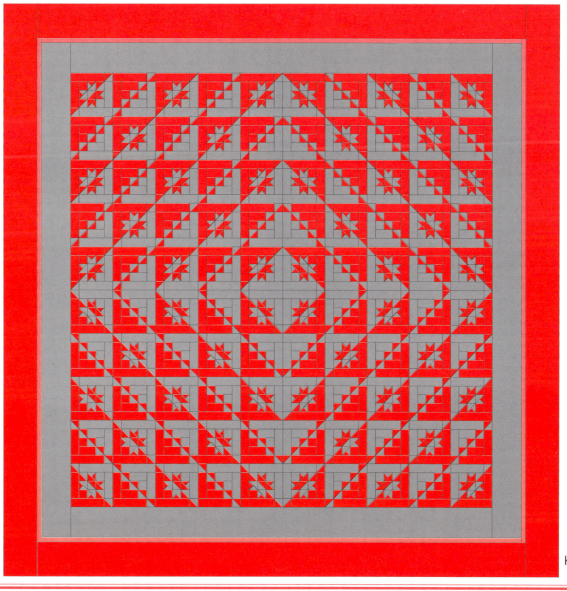

King

block 1

block 2

Lap

Barbara Morgan discovered the imaginative set in Mountain Shadows. Traditional red and white offers visual excitement and shows how dramatic this quilt design is.

YARDAGE:

	Lap 53" x 68" (6 x 8 blocks)
Light fabric	2-1/3 yds.
Dark fabric	2-7/8 yds.
Binding	5/8 yd.
Backing	3-1/4 yds.

	Queen 83" x 98" (10 x 12 blocks)
Light fabric	5-1/2 yds.
Dark fabric	6-1/4 yds.
Binding	7/8 yd.
Backing	7-1/2 yds.

CUTTING:

		Lap	
From both light & dark			
2" strips		18	
into 2" x 6-1/2"			48
2" x 5"			48
2" x 3-1/2"			16
2" x 2"			48
2-3/8" strips		2	
into 2-3/8" x 2-3/8"			32
2-3/4" strips		3	
into 2-3/4" x 2-3/4"			32
10" strips		2	
Light fabric only			
Second border 1-1/4" strips		6	
Dark fabric only			
First border 2" strips		6	
Third border 2" strips		6	
Binding 3" strips		6	

CONSTRUCTION:

MAKE HSTs according to the directions on page 4, using the chart below and the precut 10" strips of fabric.

Light/Dark	# HSTs	# rows HST paper
Lap	240	30
Queen	600	75

MAKE SUPER STAR POINT UNITS following the directions on page 5 and using all of the 2-3/8" and 2-3/4" squares. Make 64 for the Lap and 176 for a Queen.

PUT THE BLOCKS TOGETHER as instructed on page 6. The following chart shows how many of each block you'll need.

	Block #1	Block #2
Lap	32	16
Queen	88	32

USE THE DIAGRAM to arrange the blocks, then follow the General Instructions to sew them together.

SEW ON THE BORDERS as explained on page 8. Quilt and bind as discussed in the General Instructions on page 9.

Queen

| 43 |
| 120 |
| 120 |
| 32 |
| 120 |
| 6 |
| 88 |
| 6 |
| 88 |
| 5 |
| 9 |
| 9 |
| 9 |
| 9 |

Queen

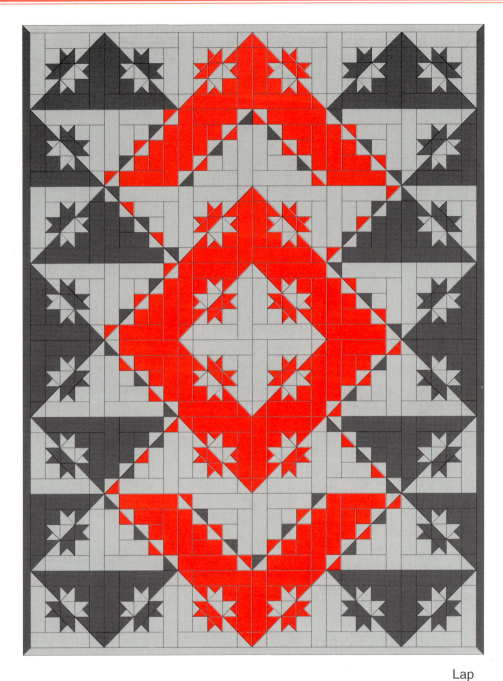

Lap

block 1

block 1 Accent

block 1

block 3

block 3a

block 4

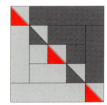

block 4a

Mary Dent chose three colors for this variation of the Mountain Shadows set. A light background and two strong dark values are lively in her spunky creation. Be creative with these blocks or reproduce Mary's creation for your friends and family to enjoy!

YARDAGE:

	Lap 45" x 60" (6 x 8 blocks)	Twin 60" x 90" (8 x 12 blocks)
Light & binding	2-5/8 yds.	5 yds.
Accent (blue) & binding	1-3/4 yds.	3 yds.
Dark (red)	1-1/8 yds.	2-1/4 yds.
Backing	2-7/8 yds.	5-1/2 yds.

CUTTING:

	Lap	Twin
Light		
2" strips	18	36
into 2" x 6-1/2"	48	96
2" x 5"	48	96
2" x 3-1/2"	16	48
2" x 2"	48	96
2-3/8" strips	3	3
into 2-3/8" x 2-3/8"	32	48
2-3/4" strips	3	5
into 2-3/4" x 2-3/4"	32	48
4-1/2" strips (binding)	3	4
10" strips	2	5
Accent		
2" strips	9	16
into 2" x 6-1/2"	24	44
2" x 5"	24	44
2" x 3-1/2"	4	12
2" x 2"	24	44
2-3/8" strips	2	2
into 2-3/8" x 2-3/8"	20	32
2-3/4" strips	2	3
into 2-3/4" x 2-3/4"	20	32
4-1/2" strips (binding)	4	5
10" strips	1	3
Dark		
2" strips	9	21
into 2" x 6-1/2"	24	52
2" x 5"	24	52
2" x 3-1/2"	12	36
2" x 2"	24	52
2-3/8" strips	1	1
into 2-3/8" x 2-3/8"	12	16
2-3/4" strips	1	2
into 2-3/4" x 2-3/4"	12	16
10" strips	1	2

CONSTRUCTION:

MAKE HSTs following the chart below. Use the directions on page 4 and the 10" strips of fabric. *Note that you will make HSTs from two color combinations.*

	# HSTs	# rows HST paper
Lap		
Light / Accent	140*	18
Light / Dark	100	13
Twin		
Light / Accent	280	35
Light / Dark	200	25

* A 10" strip of fabric will yield 136 HSTs. Since 140 HSTs are needed, use leftover fabric to cut two 2-3/8" squares of both the light and accent fabrics. Prepare four HSTs from these squares.

MAKE SUPER STAR POINT UNITS as explained on page 5 of the General Instructions. There will be both Light / Accent and Light / Dark combinations. Use the chart below to determine what you need to make for your quilt. Amounts used for the twin size will be in ( ).

Lt / Accent 20 (32) 2-3/4" squares of each color
             20 (32) 2-3/8" squares of each color
Lt / Dark   12 (16) 2-3/4" squares of each color
             12 (16) 2-3/8" squares of each color

WHEN THE COMPONENTS are cut and sewn, piece the blocks below using the General Instructions on page 6.

		Lap	Twin
Block	#1		
	Accent	20	32
	#1		
	Dark	12	16
	#3	6	18
	#3a	6	18
	#4	2	6
	#4a	2	6

ARRANGE THE BLOCKS following the drawing, then sew together using the methods on page 8.

LAYER AND QUILT. This quilt has no added border. The wide (4-1/2") binding strips form a 1" frame for the quilt.

Twin

Twinkling Mountains by Mary Dent, Durango, Co. 45" x 60"

Reflections by Sue Ann Shwiller, Durango, Co. 99" x 99"

Mountain Shadows by Barbara Morgan, Durango, Co. 53" x 68"

Reflections by Melinda Malone, Bayfield, Co. 57" x 57"

Southwestern Nights by Sue Andresen, Durango, Co. 64" x 71"

Confetti by Joan DiBlasi, Durango, Co. 60" x 90"

Stellar Eclipse by Kim Gjere, Durango, Co. 60" x 60"

Crowns in the Corner by Becky Smith, Bayfield, Co. 55" x 55"

Wallhanging

block 6   block 7

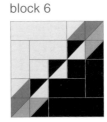  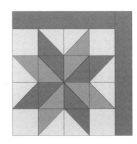

YARDAGE:

	Wallhanging 60" x 60" (4 x 4 blocks)	King 105" x 105" (10 x 10 blocks)
Light	1-1/3 yds.	4-1/3 yds.
Dark	2 yds.	6 yds.
Accent 1 (light star)	5/8 yd.	1-1/2 yds.
Accent 2 (dark star)	1-1/4 yds.	2-5/8 yds.
Binding	5/8 yd.	1 yd.
Backing	3-2/3 yds.	9-3/8 yds.

This quilt uses a combination of four fabric colors. The light value is the yellow, the dark value is the red and there is an accent color duo in the stars. The accent fabrics must be a strong contrast to the light and dark fabrics chosen. As these blocks are placed side by side, a star is formed.

25

CUTTING:

Light	Wallhanging	King
2" strips	5	28
into 2" x 5"	16	100
2" x 3-1/2"	20	136
2" x 2 "	24	80
2-1/2" strips	1	1
into 2-1/2" x 2-1/2"	16	16
3-1/2" strips	2	5
5-3/8" strips	1	5
into 5-3/8" x 5-3/8"	6	32
7" strips	1	1
10" strips	1	3

Dark	Wallhanging	King
2" strips	4	25
into 2" x 5"	16	100
2" x 3-1/2"	20	136
2" x 2"	4	36
5-3/8" strips	1	5
into 5-3/8" x 5-3/8"	6	32
9-3/4" strips	4	9
10" strips	1	3

Accent 1	Wallhanging	King
7" strip	1	1
10" strips	1	4

Accent 2	Wallhanging	King
1-3/4" strips	8	12
2" strips	4	8
7" strip	1	1
10" strips	1	4

CONSTRUCTION:

MAKE HSTs following the chart below, the directions on page 4 and using the 10" strips of fabric. Note that you will make HSTs in five different color combinations. Numbers listed first are for the wallhanging, those in parenthesis ( ) are for the king size.

Color Comb.	# HSTs		# rows HST paper	
Light / Accent 1	20	(44)	3	(6)
Dark / Accent 1	32	(200)	4	(25)
Light / Accent 2	52	(244)	7	(31)
Accent 1 / Acc 2	52	(244)	7	(31)
Light / Dark	12	(108)	2	(14)

Make Giant HSTs using the 5-3/8" squares of light and dark. Make 12 for the Wallhanging, 64 for the King.

ASSEMBLE BLOCKS following the directions in the General Instructions. Use the chart below to find out how many of each block to make.

	Block #6	Block #7
Wallhanging	4	12
King	36	64

SEW THE BLOCKS together using the drawing as a guide and following the instructions on page 8.

THE FIRST BORDER is 4-patch units* that finish the stars and connecting strips of light fabric. Begin by making 20 (44 for the King) of the 4-patch units as shown below. For each unit you need one Light / Accent 1 HST, one Light / Accent 2 HST, one Accent 1 / Accent 2 HST and one 2" square of light. The HSTs are made and the 2" squares of light have been cut. (*The 4-patch units are different, depending on the size quilt being made. Notice both illustrations.)

Lap   King

Measure the section of the quilt top on the edge between HSTs. Add 1/2" and cut the 3-1/2" strips of light into eight (twenty for the King) sections this measurement. The one shown here was 9", therefore cut 9-1/2". Yours should be close to this but because of differences in seam allowances measure before you cut.

Attach the 4-patch units to the 3-1/2" x 9-1/2" connecting strips of light fabric to complete the top and bottom borders as shown below.   (This illustration is for the wallhanging...the king simply requires more parts. See the diagram for the king for detail.)

Now make the side borders.

Attach the top and bottom borders to the quilt first, then attach the side borders.

THE SECOND BORDER is 2" strips of Accent 2.

THE THIRD BORDER WITH STAR CORNERS is a bright finish for this quilt. Make HSTs from **2"** finished paper and the 7" strips of fabrics in the quantities listed below.

	# HSTs	# rows HST paper
Light / Acct 2	16	4
Acct 1/ Acct 2	16	4
Light / Acct 1	16	4

Use sixteen 2-1/2" x 2-1/2" light squares to assemble the Star Corners as illustrated.

To two sides of the Star Corner Blocks stitch a 1-3/4" strip of the Accent 2 fabric (these two sides become the internal sides of the Star block that are then sewn to the connecting borders). See illustration. Measure the width of the quilt in the center then cut two 9-3/4" Dark strips this length (the Wallhanging measures 39-1/2").

Sew the first two wide borders to the top and bottom edges of the quilt.

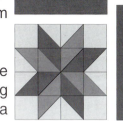

Cut two 9-3/4" Dark strips the length of the quilt (measuring through the middle). Attach a Star Corner Block to each end of these wide connecting borders, sewing the accent color strip to the wide connecting border. Attach this Star Corner Block and wide connecting border unit onto the remaining two sides of the quilt, matching corner seams.

THE FINAL BORDER uses the remaining 1-3/4" strips of Accent 2. Sew on the side edges first, then the top and bottom.

QUILT AND BIND your quilt as you wish or according to the General Instructions on page 9.

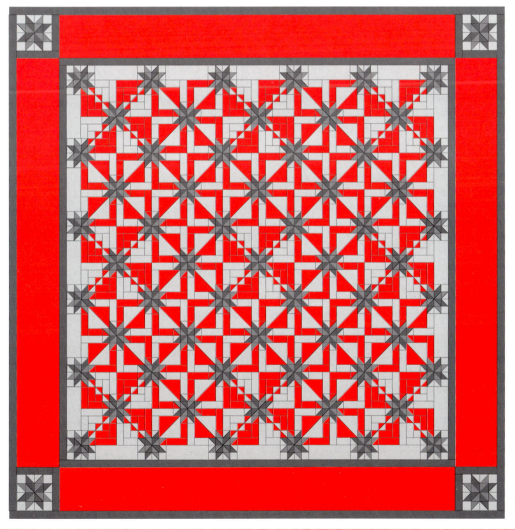

King

block 2

block 5

Wallhanging

This intriguing design is a twist of the original star block. By placing the super star point units in the corners of the block an interesting interplay between blocks is created. The two-color theme works beautifully here and the accents in the border offer visual excitement!

YARDAGE:

	Wallhanging 55" x 55 (6 x 6 blocks)	Queen 85" x 100" (10 x 12 blocks)
Light	1-3/4 yds.	5-1/4 yds.
Dark and Border #2	2-1/8 yds.	5-7/8 yds.
Border #1	1/4 yd.	1/2 yd.
Border #3	1/2 yd.	3/4 yd.
Binding	5/8 yd.	7/8 yd.
Backing	3-1/2 yds.	7-5/8 yds.

CUTTING:

	Wallhanging	Queen
Both light and dark		
2" strips	13	44
into 2" x 6-1/2"	16	60
2" x 5"	16	60
2" x 3-1/2"	76	240
2" x 2"	36	120
2-3/8" strips	2	4
into 2-3/8" x 2-3/8"	20	60
2-3/4" strips	2	4
into 2-3/4" x 2-3/4"	20	60
10 " strips	2	6
Border #1 - 1-1/2" strips	5	8
Border #2 - 2-1/4" strips (Dk)	5	9
Border #3 - 2-3/4" strips	6	9
Binding - 3" strips	6	9

CONSTRUCTION:

MAKE HSTs as explained in the General Instructions. Use the chart below and the precut 10" strips of fabric.

Light/Dark	# HSTs	# rows HST paper
Wallhanging	220	28
Queen	720	90

MAKE SUPER STAR POINT UNITS using all of the 2-3/8" and 2-3/4" squares and following the directions on page 5. Make 40 of each color for the Wallhanging and 120 of each color for the Queen size.

ASSEMBLE THE BLOCKS according to the directions on pages 6 and 7. Blocks used are:

	Block #2	Block #5
Wallhanging	16	20
Queen	60	60

SEW THE BLOCKS TOGETHER. The Pairs of Pairs method explained on page 8 is a great way to do this.

BORDERS are added next. The first border is 1-1/2" strips, border #2 is 2-1/4" strips of dark and border #3 is 2-3/4" strips. Detailed instructions of sewing borders may be found on page 8.

FINISH YOUR QUILT by quilting and binding as discussed of page 9.

Queen

C
O
N
F
E
T
T
I

block 2a

block 8

block 12

Twin

Joan DiBlasi took the blocks from Cinnamon Twist, shown on page 34, modified one, used a new set and this quilt was the result. It proves the theory that in quiltmaking there are no mistakes, just new creations!

CUTTING:

	Twin	Queen
From <u>both</u> light and dark		
2" strips	24	47
into 2" x 6-1/2"	56	116
2" x 5"	72	132
2" x 3-1/2"	40	84
2" x 2"	56	116
2-3/8" strips	2	3
into 2-3/8" x 2-3/8"	24	40
2-3/4" strips	2	3
into 2-3/4" x 2-3/4"	28	44
Light only		
2" strips	3	4
5" strips	4	5
10 " strips	4	6
Dark only		
2" strips	4	5
5" strips	3	4
10" strips	2	2
Accent		
2" strips	7	9
10" strips	2	4
Binding - 3" strips	8	10

YARDAGE:

	Twin	Queen
	60" x 90"	90" x 105"
	(6 x 10 blocks)	(10 x 12 blocks)
Light	3-7/8 yds.	6-1/4 yds.
Dark	3-1/8 yds.	4-7/8 yds.
Accent	1-1/8 yds.	1-7/8 yds.
Binding	3/4 yd.	1 yd.
Backing	5-3/8 yds.	8-1/8 yds.

CONSTRUCTION:

MAKE HSTs according to the chart below (Queen size is in parenthesis). Follow the directions on page 4.

	# HSTs	# rows HST paper
Light / Dark	144 (224)	18 (28)
Light / Accent	200 (420)	25 (53)

MAKE STAR POINT UNITS using four 2-3/4" squares of both light and dark. This will make 8 units. Directions are on page 5.

MAKE SUPER STAR POINT UNITS using the 2-3/8" squares, the remaining 2-3/4" squares and the instructions on page 5. You will make 48 (80 for the Queen) each of light and dark units.

ASSEMBLE BLOCKS following the directions and diagrams for each block in the General Instructions. You will need the blocks shown below:

	Block #2a	Block #8	Block #12
Twin	40	16	8
Queen	84	32	8

SEW THE BLOCKS together following the diagram on pages 30 and 31 with the directions for sewing Pairs of Pairs. There will be four extra #12 blocks. Set these aside to use in the border.

BORDERS are made using strip sets. First measure the width and length of your quilt as suggested under the directions for borders and note the measurement. It should be about 45-1/2" x 75-1/2" (75-1/2" x 90-1/2" for the Queen) For the longer side borders sew four (five) 2" strips of accent, the 5" strips of light and the 2" strips of dark each together, end to end, as explained for border strips in the General Instructions. Next sew these strips into a strip set as shown below, cut to the length found above, then attach to the sides of the quilt using the method for borders on page 8.

For the shorter top and bottom borders sew three (four) 2" strips of accent, the 5" strips of dark and the 2" strips of light each together. Make the strip set shown. Cut a top and bottom border from the strip set the width of the quilt as measured before the side borders were added. Attach a #12 block to each end of these short border strip sets.

Sew these borders to the top and bottom, matching seam lines where the border strips are sewn to the blocks.

YOUR QUILT is ready for quilting and binding. Additional directions for these steps may be found in the General Instructions on page 9.

Queen

Wallhanging

block 2

block 5

block 8

block 10

block 13

This quilt shows the successful combination of several of the Reflection blocks. Sue Andresen's choice of an asymmetrical set is striking!

CUTTING:

	Wallhanging	King	
From <u>both</u> light and dark			
2" strips	20	53	
into 2" x 6-1/2"	52		140
2" x 5"	52		140
2" x 3-1/2"	39		95
2" x 2"	44		126
2-3/8" strips	1	3	
into 2-3/8" x 2-3/8"	17		43
2-3/4" strips	2	3	
into 2-3/4" x 2-3/4"	17		43
5-3/8" strip	1	1	
into 5-3/8" x 5-3/8"	2		2
10" strips	4	8	
Light only			
3-3/8" strips	3	5	
into 3-3/8" x 3-3/8"	30		60
Dark only			
2-1/2" strips	13	19	
3-3/8" strips	3	5	
into 3-3/8" x 3-3/8"	28		58
Binding - 3" strips	7	10	

YARDAGE:

	Wallhanging	King
	64" x 71"	102" x102"
	(7 x 8 blocks)	(12 x 12 blocks)
Light	3-1/4 yds.	7 yds.
Dark	4-1/4 yds.	8-1/3 yds.
Binding	2/3 yd.	1 yd.
Backing	3-7/8 yds.	9-1/8 yds.

CONSTRUCTION:

MAKE HSTs according to the General Instructions in the amounts below. Use the 10" strips of light and dark.

Light / Dark	# HSTs	# rows HST paper
Wallhanging	444	4
King	1,036	8

MAKE FOUR GIANT HSTs using the 5-3/8" squares of light and dark.

MAKE SUPER STAR POINT UNITS as described on page 5. Use all of the 2-3/8" and 2-3/4" squares. These will make 34 each of light and dark units for the Lap and 86 each for the King.

MAKE THE BLOCKS as directed in the General Instructions. The following blocks are needed:

Block	#2	#5	#8	#10	#13
Wallhanging	27	4	13	8	4
King	83	4	39	14	4

ARRANGE THE BLOCKS using the drawing as a guide, then sew using the Pairs of Pairs method described on page 8.

THE BORDER on this quilt takes more time than most but the result is worth it. The first border is simply 2-1/2" strips of dark sewn to all four sides. Follow the directions on page 8 to avoid rippling on the edges.

For the second border use the remaining HSTs and the 3-3/8" squares of light and dark. These 3-3/8" squares must first be cut into quarters diagonally.

Begin by sewing a light triangle to a HST then to a dark triangle. Make 112 (232 for the King) units like this:

For the two short sides sew 26 of these units together to form each border strip. Sew 30 of these units together for each long side. Since the King is square you will need four border strips, each made from 58 of these units. *Note: Due to variations in seam allowances, your border may require one or two more or fewer of these units.*
To complete the border strip, sew two light triangles onto one HST. Then sew this corner unit onto the right end of each border strip.

Pin border strips to the quilt, matching the center of the strips to the center of the sides. Be careful not to stretch the border. Sew border on, starting and stopping 1/4" from edge. Miter the border strips together where they meet at the corners.

A final 2-1/2" dark border is added.

QUILT AND BIND the quilt as you wish, or follow the suggestions in the General Instructions on page 9.

King

Topper

This Americana style quilt features pinwheels, stars and a decorative border that create the rustic warmth and charm that many of our grandmothers' quilts had! It puzzles the eye with its asymmetrical layout. Sure to please old quilt fanciers and modern day quilt admirers alike, this quilt was made by Melinda Malone. Special thanks to Barbara Morgan for the fun border!

block 2a   block 8a   block 14a

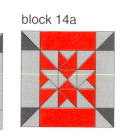

YARDAGE:

	Topper 81" x 81" (8 x 8 blocks)
Light	5-1/4 yds.
Dark (red)	2-1/2 yds.
Accent (blue)	2-3/8 yds.
Binding	3/4 yd.
Backing	5 yds. *

*Very tight! If the fabric is any less than 44" in width, 7-1/3 yds. is better.

CUTTING:

Light	Topper	
1-1/2" strips	15	
2" strips	28	
into 2" x 6-1/2"		56
2" x 5"		72
2" x 3-1/2"		40
2" x 2"		56
2-3/8" strips	2	
into 2-3/8" x 2-3/8"		24
2-3/4" strips	2	
into 2-3/4" x 2-3/4"		28
3" strips	1	
into 3" x 3"		8
5-1/2" strips	5	
into 5-1/2" x 5-1/2"		32
10" strips	5	

Dark		
2" strips	24	
into 2" x 6-1/2"		56
2" x 5"		72
2" x 3-1/2"		40
2" x 2"		56
2-3/8" strips	2	
into 2-3/8" x 2-3/8"		24
2-3/4" strips	2	
into 2-3/4" x 2-3/4"		28
10" strips	2	

Accent		
2" strips	4	
2-1/2" strips	6	
3" strips	8	
10" strips	3	

Binding - 3" strips	8	

CONSTRUCTION:

MAKE HSTs according to the directions on page 4, using the chart below and the precut 10" strips of fabric.

	# HSTs	# rows HST paper
Light / Dark	176	22
Light / Accent	280	35

MAKE EIGHT STAR POINT UNITS according to the General Instructions on page 5 and using four 2-3/4" squares each of light and dark.

MAKE SUPER STAR POINT UNITS using the remaining 2-3/4" squares, the 2-3/8" squares and following the directions on page 5.

ASSEMBLE BLOCKS as explained in the block construction section of the General Instructions. The following blocks are needed.

Block	#2a	#8a	#14a
Quantity	40	16	8

When the blocks are completed lay them out following the drawing of the quilt. The quarters of this quilt are identical with each quarter being turned 1/4 of a turn to get the pinwheel effect. (NOTE: There is a slight difference between the drawing of the quilt and the photograph. The drawing illustrates the quilt with each quarter being identical. The photographed quilt is the same except that all the corner blocks are turned the same direction.) Sew the blocks together, referring to the General Instructions on page 8.

BORDERS ARE ADDED to the quilt top. The 1st, 2nd, 4th and 5th borders are all plain border strips. Sew them on according to the directions on page 8. The first border is 2-1/2" strips of accent. The second border is 1-1/2" strips of light.

The 3rd border is the pinwheel border. Each side of the pinwheel border consists of six pinwheels and ten 4-patch units.

Border Pinwheels

1. Make 24 pinwheels from Light / Dark HSTs. Half should look like those on the left and the rest like those on the right.

2. Make four pinwheels from light / accent HSTs, two spinning one way and two spinning the opposite way.

4-patch units - make 40

1. Using four 2" strips of light and four 2" strips of accent sew four Light / Accent strip sets.
2. Press to the darker strips.
3. Segment into 2" pieces.
4. To make a 4-patch unit, take two segments, place with opposite colors facing right sides together and sew together.

Connecting background pieces

1. Cut the 5-1/2" squares of light into quarters, diagonally.

Lay out the border blocks. The pattern is pinwheel, 4-patch, 4-patch, pinwheel, 4-patch, 4-patch, pinwheel ..... until six pinwheels and ten 4-patch units are used on each side of the quilt. *Note: The pinwheels alternate.* At this point leave off the end Light / Accent pinwheels. We'll come back and pick them up later.

Lay down the connecting light triangles so the bias edges are toward the pieced blocks and the straight of grain edge to the outside. Stitch two connecting triangles to the ends of all pinwheel and 4-patch blocks. Set aside the end dark pinwheels on two sides (four pinwheels) with the accent pinwheels.

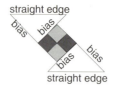

Sew these units together to make the borders, taking care to match the blocks at the seam line.

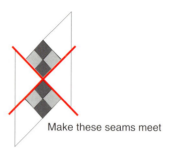

Make these seams meet

Cut the eight 3" squares of light in half diagonally. These triangles are used on the end pinwheels so the edges will be on the straight of grain, not bias. Eight pinwheels, four dark and four accent have been set aside. Use the corner triangles just cut, the larger triangles used to connect the border blocks and these pinwheels to make two of the following units from each color. Add them now to the appropriate ends, using the drawing as a guide.

2 like this   2 like this   2 like this   2 like this

Stitch the short borders on opposite sides of the quilt, using the drawing to see which way the pinwheels spin. Add the long borders to the remaining edges. The dark pinwheels should be next to the accent pinwheels in the corners. Match their points.

Sew on the 4th border, which is 1-1/2" strips of light.

Add the final border, 3" strips of accent.

SEE THE GENERAL INSTRUCTIONS for quilting and binding directions on page 9.

Lap

block 8

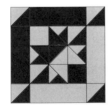
block 9

block 10

block 11

Kim Gjere selected four blocks, then presented them in strong contrasting fabrics. Take a close look at the print in her quilt. It's a great idea to use a lively printed fabric to create a dramatic effect!

YARDAGE:

	Lap 60" x 60" (6 x 6 blocks)	Twin 60" x 90" (6 x 10 blocks)
Light	2-1/3 yds.	4 yds.
Dark	2-3/4 yds.	4-3/8 yds.
Binding	5/8 yd.	3/4 yd.
Backing	3-2/3 yds.	5-1/2 yds.

37

CUTTING:

From both light and dark:	Lap	Twin
2" strips	11	18
into 2" x 6-1/2"	24	48
2" x 5"	40	64
2" x 3-1/2"	8	8
2" x 2"	20	32
2-3/8" strips	2	2
into 2-3/8" x 2-3/8"	20	32
2-3/4" strips	2	3
into 2-3/4" x 2-3/4"	20	32
5-3/8" strips	1	1
into 5-3/8" x 5-3/8"	4	4
10" strips	2	4
Light only		
8" strips	2	4
Dark only		
8" strips	4	6
Binding		
3" strips	6	8

CONSTRUCTION:

MAKE HSTs according to the General Instructions on page 4. You'll need the quantities shown below:

Light/Dark	# HSTs	# rows HST paper
Lap	244	31
Twin	436	55

Make eight Giant HSTs using the 5-3/8" squares of light and dark.

MAKE SUPER STAR POINT UNITS. Refer to page 5 in the General Instructions. Use all of the 2-3/4" and 2-3/8" squares and make 40 each of the light and dark units for the Lap, 64 each for theTwin.

BLOCKS CAN NOW BE ASSEMBLED. The General Instructions will tell you in detail how to make each of the blocks listed below. Make the quantity needed for your quilt.

BLOCK	#8	#9	#10	#11
Lap	16	4	8	8
Twin	28	4	20	8

SEW THE BLOCKS together using the Pairs of Pairs method described on page 8.

DECORATIVE BORDER:

Layer two 8" strips of dark fabric with <u>right sides together</u>. Cut off selvage and cut as shown.

Repeat with two additional strips.

Layer two 8" strips light fabric with <u>right sides together</u> and cut following the drawing below. For the twin size repeat this step with two additional

strips of light and with two strips of dark.

Sew two short borders and two long borders.

Short Border *

Long Border *

*Twin borders have an extra dark and light strip on each side of center.

Sew short borders to the top and bottom first, matching seams as necessary, then trim ends even with the quilt top. Sew the long borders to the sides, again matching seams and trimming ends.

FOLLOW THE General Instructions on page 9 for quilting and binding your quilt.